AF609235

GOYA

Get Off Your A$$

JEREMY D. JACKSON

Printed and Bound in the United States of America

ISBN: 978-0-578-84140-3 (Print)

First printing January 2021

Front cover photography:
Donald Pigford

Editing, book cover, and interior design:
Jessica Tilles/TWA Solutions
www.twasolutions.com

Table of Contents

Introduction

Welcome to G.O.Y.A. This book will enlighten you on how to perceive the world through a different lens. Raised in a city where mindsets are trapped and beaten, I never desired to travel in the same lane as others. You're reading this book, so I know you feel the same way. I always viewed life distinctively. Even though I grew up in such a unique place, I learned how to alter my mindset. You don't have to change who you are, just the way you go about doing things. I have split personalities that I've learned to flick on and off. The personalities comprise the "Memphis me" attitude and the "real me" mentality. I only said this to say, it's all right to keep the mindset you have because it benefits you. However, there are also opportunities to develop a different concept that will help you build and grow. I've already received undeniable results and success because of these methods. My focus is to help you become untrapped.

First, I would like to thank you for supporting me. Great feelings take over my body when I know I'm helping someone that feels the same way I do. Mastering control over your life is an everyday journey. The mirror is your best friend and you must stay true to it. The change you're looking for, I have planted into this book strategically, and just like everything else in this world, it's up to you to take control.

I created this book to break down the steps that will allow you to realize you're in control of your own life. Everyone, at some point, says to themselves:

- I need a change.
- I can't continue to live this way.
- I want better.

I'm here to express to you it's one hundred percent possible. Most times, our brains are too stubborn to allow us to adjust, so therefore, I ask you to read with an open mind. Open your mind to new ways, and you will see new opportunities that you were once blind to.

G.O.Y.A will be your guide. I will teach you how to gain control, develop self-confidence, have self-discipline, become successful, and much more. All I ask is for you to comprehend this method, be open-minded, and apply it. This new way of thinking allowed me to maneuver through challenges and look at life from a fresh perspective.

If you believe life consists of luck and not hard work, then this book is for you. Although, throw that assumption into the nearest dumpster. I will teach you how to work smart, gain mental stability, and not rely on luck. Follow my instructions and the methods listed in this book. Once again, I thank you for reading this self-help book. You are leading your life in the right direction.

Don't Be a Meal

When you're sitting at your dinner table with an appetite the size of a lion, your meal doesn't have a chance in this world to survive. Don't be that meal, because that's the exact way it is if you allow life to make you its lunch.

Often, living becomes a burden, and life forces you to make tough decisions. Life is continuous, so it becomes a nonstop battle. It's tiring, and it seems as if the only option is to give up. Wrong! Fight until you can't, tomorrow can just as well be the day you make it over the mountain.

To not be a meal, you must have a strong mindset. There should be little to no indecisiveness in your mentality. It's easy to throw excuses into your life, in which your excuses could be facts. Even so, it's an excuse and it can turn you into a scrumptious meal for life to gobble you up. Life has its way of weighing on your shoulders. Life waits until you're vulnerable and then takes advantage of your mind. Here are a few ways you can avoid being a meal.

#1 Seize procrastination

#1 Delete your troubling past

#1 Lose your bad habits

#1 Run from Irrelevant information

Seize Procrastination

Procrastination is the root of all evil in being successful. It's impossible to sit on your ass and accomplish the goals you have set for yourself. In reaching expectations of your own, it takes resilience and persistence. Both terms deal with breaking through a tough wall to get to the checkpoint. Listen carefully, you never actually reach the finish line. Your finish line is a mirage that will keep moving further away from you. This is a gift and a curse. If you're a hustler, you'll keep chasing your perception to reach happiness. A smart person will fall in love with the grind and find success and happiness at your checkpoints. Procrastination will leave you in a pit of regret because you will accomplish nothing.

Delete Your Troubling Past

This is important because your past has a lot to do with your progression in life. Majority of the time you allow the negatives of your past to invade your promising future. Delete your troubling past and forget about it. This is the last day you should let your past stunt your growth.

Allowing the past to sit between you and your success is selfish and self-inflicting. Don't hold yourself back because you have no clue what type of effect the past has on you. Stop allowing where you come from, the people you grew up with, and past failures hold you back. Grow up, turn every negative into a positive, and be successful.

Lose Your Bad Habits

Bad habits distract you from what's important on your journey. There are three things bad habits do to your life. The three D's: distract, delay, and detour. The D's create unforeseen circumstances that slow down your ETA. These are only circumstances, continue on your journey and fight through the hardships of life. Bad habits are only temporary enjoyments that make it hard for you to progress.

Run From Irrelevant Information

Ignore, run, jog, flee, or whatever you need to do to get away from worthless information. In the social media age, there are record numbers of irrelevant information at your fingertips. Although irrelevant information can't harm you physically, it definitely can affect your mentality. Everyone else's opinion can and will alter how you think.

Surround yourself with people who are going to be helpful to your growth, not people who enjoy gossiping and filled with drama. Most people enjoy just hanging, which isn't a bad thing when you thrive on being a social being. When you're attempting to achieve greatness, there isn't time to just hang every day. Find people looking to learn and improve, just like you.

Risk Must Be Taken

When you decide you want to be successful, you understand you must take risks to achieve certain goals. Now, what I want to reiterate to you is concerning dumb and smart risk. You never want to trick yourself out of your position. If it's a chance that you might lose everything, that's a dumb risk. A smart risk is much easier to comprehend. You're not putting everything on odds. There's a way to calculate a good risk. If you're going to lose more than you put up, then that might be a poor decision.

It's important to have great risk-reward management when taking chances. You don't want to lose everything you've worked for on one crazy mistake. Learn how to take a calculated risk. It'll pay off for you. Discipline yourself, because one ignorant risk could put you twenty steps backward. Studying and researching decreases the likelihood of being on the wrong side of risk.

When you're destined to be successful, there's no reason you should be afraid to take risks. If you're too timid to take a risk, you do not want to be as successful as you think. The only thing that's stopping you from leveling up is fear. You will never know what's on the other side of fear unless you take risks. Don't allow made up outcomes to stop you from witnessing the real outcome. F.E.A.R equals: False evidence appearing real.

Here's how to change the way you feel about taking a risk. First, get off your ass and take the risk! It's the only way to become comfortable with chances. Study more than enough on the subject that you're involved in. Take a well-calculated risk that you feel comfortable with and equip yourself with the knowledge you need to achieve. Fear is only an illusion that can leave you contempt and stagnant in life. Take that risk and see your real potential.

Failure Will Happen

If I haven't mentioned it before, I'll do so again. Being great and getting off your ass isn't something many people can accomplish. Why? Because it's hard as hell to stay consistent and put in work daily. That's exactly what you have to do to achieve the goals you have set for yourself. Some days are easier than others, but the key thing is that you must get started. So, get off your ass today.

When a person thinks of failure, they think of the worse feeling possible. A year ago, I read a book that revealed strategies on how to perceive failure in a different light. Since then, my mindset has been different. This mindset toward failure changed my entire perception of life. Instead of failure slowing me down, it became a way to speed me up.

Failure does not mean stop. Instead of allowing failure to wound you, you must allow it to assist you. When failure happens, that means it's time to figure out "the why." Ask yourself:

- Why did I fail?
- What should I do differently next time?
- Maybe I did it wrong, let me try again.

It's about trial and error. You must go through failure to get to the results you're so desperately seeking. That's why giving up should be evicted from your brain every time it enters.

Due to the effect that failure has on most people, it's tough to even fathom the thought of allowing failure to help you move forward. Most don't even try new things because they're afraid they will potentially fail. To gain the confidence to begin, you must first prepare yourself. If you are not fully equipped, you are going to have tension and doubt. Do yourself a favor and prepare for the situation. That comes from research, reading, and experience.

Research

You have a lot of questions, and you need direction in your field of choice. Researching your questions can be an easy way for you to gather information. Not all information will be worthy, but that's where distinctiveness comes into the equation. Take advantage of the many tools to assist you, because you won't be able to rely on the next person to give you all the information. Researching information teaches you how to grasp valuable material you can use to benefit yourself.

Read

Reading is fundamental. Just like you're reading now, you're gaining another perspective. Different perspectives help you whether or not you know it. Read books that water your purpose. It's cool to read other books but attempt to build your library with words that move you closer to fulfilling your gift. You are in control of what you read.

Experience

Experience gives you the knowledge you can't get from anywhere else. For me, experience has been my greatest teacher. When I don't accomplish what I set out to, I examine and recap the entire experience many times. When we go through experiences, we gain knowledge that strengthens us. You know what to expect now, you gain different alerts that will trigger you, and mentally you have options to choose from. With experience, you know what works and what doesn't.

Like success, failure is mental. What you perceive is what you get. Don't expect to have a negative outlook and still receive good news. To attract positivity, you must exert that energy to the world. If you're like me, you feel you only can succeed if you put the work in. It's correct that we have to work hard, but it's time to only use your mind. Orchestrate it, find structure, be persistent with your purpose, and complete tasks.

Give yourself a task that will benefit growth toward your purpose. Use your experiences, work smart, think outside of the box, and never limit yourself. Without failure, I wouldn't know this. Be the CEO of your life and you will achieve success through failure.

Pain

One of the reasons you're here searching for answers is because of pain. Being able to channel your pain is a very critical aspect of growing in life. There are things you must know about yourself when dealing with this sharp feeling. Let's get one thing clear, pain is a universal emotion. Yes, it does hurt, and most times we even question if it's possible to even endure. Yes, it is. Pain has its levels, but that doesn't mean it's undefeatable.

At any time during this piece, you feel like I'm being unrealistic, that's not the case. You can believe anything is possible or you believe that the impossible is just that—impossible. We must believe wholeheartedly that things are within our reach. Believing means we have faith, and when we have faith, there's no question that it will happen.

Like the famous quote says, "Whether you think you can, or you think you can't—you're right."

There are two kinds of pain I recognize—the sharpest and the lightest. The lightest pain comes from the losses we can recover from, the simple mistakes we overlooked because we weren't focused, and the pain from our perfectly painted expectations. Many people might consider things to be a loss, but I look at it for the lesson it is. I'm not speaking to my simple-minded readers who believe in the word can't and love to make excuses just because they can. No, I'm talking to those who can open their eyes through pain and think improvement. Transform every loss into a lesson, and you will think a different way.

If you have a passion for what you do, those simple mistakes get to you. It's somewhat painful; it hurts because you know you could've been more focused. It's as if that mistake continuously pokes you until you go back to fix it. Once you analyze what went wrong, refocus, and do not make the same mistake again.

Have you ever visualized how something could go? It feels so real, it's beautiful, you can even grab it almost, then poof, it doesn't go that way at all. That hurt! Too many times I found myself creating expectations on things I couldn't control. It's all right to look forward to a certain outcome, but you must realistically believe it can go a different direction. Creating expectations sets the bar high, and it's hard to top that. When you can control it, it's fine to expect a certain outcome. However, if there's no real control, expect the unexpected.

The sharpest pain comes from an unexpected death, heartbreak, and failure. Sharp pain is by far the trickiest feeling in the universe. Sharp pain lingers. It's extremely painful, it weighs you down, and it has your soul miserable as if life is ending. Either way we group pain, your circumstances will dictate the level of the pain you will feel. This is the exact moment your strength should kick in. With death, it's all right to mourn, heartbreaks take time to get over, and we need to learn from failures. I'm here to explain that the strategy of overcoming is created amid this storm called pain. The length of the hurt is unknown, but you're in control.

To move on from pain, it takes action. If you're waiting for something magical to happen, you will forever wait. With action, you improve your situation instead of masking it. Don't get me wrong. If you like to hope things get better, that's on you. Sure, you feel good for the moment, and everything is temporarily all right. What will you do when that medicine wears off? If it's hard for you to take action, don't give up on yourself. You're not the only one. Action sounds like a simple step to take, but it's not. If pain is holding you back from succeeding, you've come to the right place. Let us improve our thinking.

Focus on advancing. You must learn to face pain eye to eye. For you to grow and move through life, you must challenge pain like it's challenging you. The key to growing through pain is being able to channel your emotions. You can channel pain by forgetting it even exist or find a healthy coping mechanism. As we all may know, bottling up pain and trying to act like it's not there is dangerous. Which, in the long run, could hurt you and those around you.

The way I deal with pain is indescribable. Some will say I'm putting a cap on my pain, but I don't look at it that way. For example, death hurts as bad as anything I can describe. It affects me, but my drive is to move forward in life. Three of the most important people passed away recently, and my heart is aching as I type because I miss them. I love them all, and because of that, I push forward. I use the memories we shared as gas on my journey. Don't let pain stand in the way of your progress. That's all I'm saying.

I'm not saying you won't feel pain. Know that pain is an emotion, so it's a way to overcome it. I've learned to look at myself from a different perspective when I go through overwhelming things. Looking at myself as if I weren't me opened my eyes, and made me realize I'm just another human being with emotions. As you view your life through another lens, you're mentally preparing yourself to achieve the unknown. Later, in the following chapters, we're going to dive into what preparation looks like and how it will lead to your accomplishing more goals and being successful.

What's Success?

This is the question you should ask yourself before anything. What's success? I label success as the ability to accomplish the goals you set. Your definition of success shouldn't be an image of another person's life. That perception only drives you backward. Only the definition you create will truly make you happy along your journey.

The perception of success is dangerous if good intentions don't follow. Are your intentions in line with your morals? How long would it take to reach this success? What are your plans after success? What does your success look like? Asking yourself these questions will help you avoid going down the wrong path and will, most definitely, assist with finding your true success.

Making sure your intentions are in line with your morals is fairly simple. The things you believe in will reflect a perfect image of what your success will look like. Remember, your success isn't anyone else's success. For example, a person could perceive you as successful, but in your reality, you're nowhere near your goals. Stick to what you know to reach your happiness. So, never get caught up in another person's view of you. Only focus on your own.

One thing I would like to mention about perception is that it can make or break you. Truly becoming focused on your goals can save you from a road of misery. Being focused eliminates the belief of different opinions and personal thoughts. It's important not to fall for the opinions of others. Everyone doesn't have the best interest in mind for you.

You also must protect yourself from personal thoughts of your own. When we're overwhelmed, distracted, and moody, our thoughts become negative. You must know these are only unwanted thoughts caused by stress. Your unwanted thoughts will detour your plans and have you going in the wrong direction. Do NOT believe your mind when you're reacting off emotion. Operating off emotion will destroy your dreams before anybody else can. React off logic, and you will rarely regret your decisions. Success comes from control. Find it!

Let's take a turn to focus on your ETA. Yes, your estimated time of arrival. How long is it going to take you to reach your success? If you don't have the answer to that question, truly strategize and get on your journey toward your destination. Simply create a plan that you will operate by and stick to it. Of course, we never know when our dreams will blossom, but our success is up to us to accomplish.

Your ETA is more important than you realize. Your ETA will continue to get pushed back if there is procrastination present. I hate to break a couple of hearts, but it's needed. Excuses will delay your ETA. Poor relationships will delay your arrival time. Drugs, partying, social media, and other distractions will have your ETA set to never. You're in control of your ETA, and if you let simple distractions detour you off your journey, you'll never reach your destination. No one cares about the reason you can't do something, because nothing will happen for you if you constantly allow excuses to sit you down. Focus and fuck excuses.

Okay now, it's important to plan out every single detail. You always want to be better prepared as you can be. That's why you also should focus on what will come after you reach your destination. Success is a great feeling. Well, for about three minutes and then your mind wants more. What will be your next move? Know these things, so you won't lose time planning at that moment. It's better to adjust your plans than to be stuck planning at the moment with pressure added.

Success is what you make it. Allow yourself to feel this great feeling of accomplishment. It comes from hard work, and unfortunately, there's no way around it. Focus and commit to being disciplined. You don't want to regret not working hard when life is coming to an end. We don't have the same life as anyone else. Take control of your life, and a lot more things will happen in your favor. Focus and fuck excuses.

Prepare

Repeat after me. Prior planning prevents poor performance. Prior planning prevents poor performance. Prior planning prevents poor performance. Now, think of a time that you planned versus a time that you didn't. Ninety-nine percent of the time, if you plan, the results will be in your favor. But I can also hear you screaming at me, saying, "I've done great before without planning." "I've planned before and it didn't help." I didn't say it was impossible to succeed without planning. Why wouldn't you want the odds more in your favor with planning? If you planned and it didn't work out, work harder on planning and executing. Instead of moving backward, looking for excuses, work forward. If relying on luck is your way to get through life, I'm going to need you to get a better mindset, point blank period. Why play with your life like it ain't real? The best even practice and prepare every day. What makes you different? Oh yeah, they're where they worked to be and you're not.

If a person wants to be great, the path isn't nice or easy. Being mentally stronger to endure the many obstacles that are ahead. Knowing obstacles are a part of the game of life, you must be prepared. Preparing yourself takes patience and observance, and is required for your planning. Grab a planner from your nearest market and jot down your goals. Know your weaknesses, your strengths, and study what it takes to make your goals accomplished. If you didn't already know that a strategic process is what it takes to progress your journey, then I hope you're taking this information well. I will not be easy on you. I'm hard on myself or those around me. If you're soft mentally, accomplishing goals are not for you. Be a couch potato.

Be passionate! Being passionate is a part of loving what you do, such as knowing the seriousness of your job and doing it in a certain way. Yes, the being passionate side effect is that you could get hurt sometimes, but being passionate is what drives you. You should focus on nothing, but bringing your dreams into a reality. You cannot fake having passion; it has to be in you. It brings out the best in you. If it doesn't bring out the best in you, stop right now while you have time.

A smart way to prepare is to do so strategically. It sort of feels like you're preparing for a boxing match, and you have to withstand twelve rounds—in our case, it's twelve months. Does a boxer only prepare for a one-round fight? No, and if he or she does, they're in big trouble. It's too many outcomes that could occur and a lot of obstacles we have to go through to survive. The obstacles don't have to be huge, as most times they're small and small obstacles need just as much attention.

Being able to observe detail is a vital skill you need. Most people skip the phase to observe, and it hurts in the long run. You find answers and you feel. It's important to feel the moment to test your instincts. Check if your instincts are on point, listen to what your gut tells you, and be in tune with your inner self. In everything there's detail, make it a priority to search for it. Give everything life, nothing is too small to prepare for.

I can't stress enough how important it is for you to focus your mindset while trying to achieve a goal. I know it gets tiring but that's just how the game goes. Prepare yourself to last long, not to just hit a home run and call it a day. Longevity is the reason we work so hard to reach the top. When you reach the top, it will be another top you will have to reach.

Here's how to prepare for a twelve-month boxing match.

- Find your goal
- Your motive must be strong
- Give yourself relevant tasks every day
- List weaknesses and improve them
- Educate yourself on your opponents (the specific industry you want to achieve in, and the other opponent is life)
- Form a routine
- Be strategic
- Play to win

When you find your actual goal, there should be less questioning yourself and more knowing. You're super focused, so it's easy to understand what's for you and what will lead you in the right direction. You should lock your goal in and never keep altering it.

Your motive keeps you from giving up. If your motive is weak, you will happily give in to pressure. When your foundation is strong, you're able to build. Then again, if it's weak, it'll crumble.

The task you set for yourself should be attainable and not overwhelming. A lot of us make the mistake of overloading our lives. This might seem as if you're focused and want to accomplish goals, but sometimes, overloading can kill your work ethic. Be realistic; effectiveness is the big key to being successful. Effectiveness leads to a positive pattern.

It's easy to overlook your weaknesses when trying to be successful. In all actuality, you need your weaknesses to be successful. The first line of business is to list your weaknesses and be aware of them. Get over being afraid of your own weaknesses or else you'll never improve and get over any obstacle. It takes someone with fire in their eyes to be successful and do what's needed to reach the top. So, don't be afraid of your small weaknesses, just improve them. Once you have your weaknesses out in the open, the next step is to work on strengthening them. This will indeed make you a better person. Accept the challenge!

If it's serious enough, be one step ahead. Educate yourself on your opponents: the industry you're trying to excel in, and your life. Preparation is a must. Being educated allows you to become immune to the ignorance that could keep you at a halt.

Think of a time when you thought you could never get past a certain situation. After some time passed and you educated yourself, you zoomed past that situation with no difficulty. That's what educating yourself will get you.

Educate yourself on the mental aspect of life. The reason majority of people don't last in accomplishing goals is because they're easily distracted by adversity. Developing a strong mental will help you through the difficulties of life.

Program your mind to be great through repetition. It's a select few that can just wing life and be successful. If you're not one of those people, form a routine you can stick with. Just like a manager at a business, plan and give yourself orders on what to do to get the job done.

Know how you plan to execute. Never go into anything without a strategic plan. Appear to be one way but give them something totally different. Seem calm on the outside but be so passionate on the inside. Be unpredictable and knock life off balance with your own strategic way.

Never go into a match playing not to lose. Realistically, you've already lost if that's your mindset. What's the reason for doing anything if you don't think you will be successful? Drop the fear of losing and gain the obsession to win. Give it your all and you'll never lose.

COURAGE

"It's all right to fear change buts it's not all right not to have courage."

The definition of courage is the ability to do something that frightens you. Let me be the first to tell you—you're not the only person who has fears. Once upon a time, my greatest fear was failure. My perception of losing was as toxic as the mindset given to me as a child. No one taught us the benefits that failure brings. We're only surrounded by the negative aspects. To gain courage, you must first stop being afraid of your fear and look at it directly. Learn why your fears bother you.

I will thoroughly explain the mirror method later in the book, but as of now, follow these instructions. Find a mirror and stare into it. Ask yourself, "Are my fears holding me back from the life I want?" If the answer is yes, congratulations! You're being true to yourself. Let's say your answer was no. That's fine; continue to read with an open mind.

Gaining courage comes from one major key: accountability! Once you're able to understand that another human has nothing to do with your progress, you will then grow. You have to comprehend that if you do not reach your goal, it's no one's fault but your own. Most people have a lot on their plates, but in all actuality, if you want to accomplish anything, you will find a way. If you don't, your circumstances become your excuse. Don't allow an excuse to turn into your lifelong sacrifice. You will either sacrifice time to get your goal or your goal will be the sacrifice. Look inside yourself. Doing so will grow your accountability and allow you to find a solution to your problems.

As I continued to play life safe, I noticed other people not giving a fuck about the decisions they made. I always thought of this approach as careless and nonstrategic until I purposely paid attention to what I now call the not-giving-a-fuck technique. It's a genius approach, but for this approach to be successful, you will need courage. Even though it seems like a careless approach, it's a tactic you must add to your repertoire. Allow your mind to open and accept new strategies. No, I didn't say forget everything you ever knew. I only said, "Allow your mind to open and accept new strategies."

Because of the not-giving-a-fuck technique, I found a balance. I quickly understood that I couldn't perceive a different outcome unless I did something a tad bit different. You might have heard the saying, "The same keys don't unlock new doors." Digest this statement and gain meaning from it. Creating meaning for yourself allows you to create motives and notions. Two doors will open from this method: challenges and failure.

In case you didn't notice, challenges are an everyday thing. Look around you, everything in this world presents a challenge for you to overcome. Having a spouse, a job, a business, being in college, sports, etc. Challenges are everywhere like the air. Searching for meaning in simple statements like "The same keys don't unlock new doors" prepares you for these challenges. Through meaning, you will find life. Trust me, through this vision, challenges will seem natural to take on.

Now, let's talk about the scariest monster of them all. Failure! First, let's quickly change the negative mindset we have about failure. Failure is only scary to those who feel as if it's the end. Reprogram your mindset to view it as the total opposite. Look at it as being the beginning. Let me help you out. See, I look at failure as the beginning because now I have answers. Failure presents you with the answers you need to succeed. Failing provides some with a bad taste in their mouths. But understand it's only bitter when a person doesn't know how to use failure to their advantage. Once you fail, incorporate this method. After you receive failure, dissect the situation closely. Instead of blaming others or looking for sympathy, learn what went wrong. Improve those areas and come back stronger. Next time you face that obstacle, it won't even phase you. Failure is a part of the cheat code—use it or let it use you.

I'm only here to enlighten you on the controls you have. You must tap into what you already have. I never enjoyed taking risks. At an early age, I decided I'll play every situation safely. That will not get you the life you dream of. For the longest I allowed other people to project their contagious doubts onto my life. I thought if I played it safe, I would get rewarded. I was wrong. Instead, absolutely nothing happened but the norm. Developing courage is the first step to evolve your life. Allow yourself to engrave that definition deep into your brain. Revisit it and read it over and over until you are fearless.

There's a story of a boy we all know. The boy who lived on his stoop. He played on his stoop, ate lunch on his stoop, exercised, and even slept on his stoop. Anything you can name he did while being right there on his old rugged stoop. People would invite him to places and ask him to join them for the company, but he never left his stoop. Only this one bright day his life changed. The stoop boy noticed a young lady across the street he found very attractive. Every day, the stoop boy would imagine how life would be if he was with her. For days, months, and even years he would drool over what he thought was the most beautiful person in the world. He was so infatuated with the life he created in his mind, he missed out on doing one thing. Actually, taking action! He didn't have the courage to try anything new. Going a different direction from the norm frightened him, even if it meant receiving the woman of his dreams, which he never pursued because of being stuck in his closed mindset.

This happens every day around us. The stoop boy is in all of us. Having strong aspirations are only great if you act on them. Things hardly ever just fall into your lap. Have the courage to go get what's yours. If you believe it, you can achieve it. Most say, "I'll see it when I believe it." That's not the smartest mindset to have. Find the closest mirror and say, "I must believe it to see it!"

The Same Keys Won't Open Different Doors

This is a mistake that everyone must overcome. It could be your effort or even the dedication that you give, but don't, for one second, believe you can open different doors with the same keys you already have. It might sound redundant to mention, but there are a lot of closed-minded people who believe old keys will open new doors. The more you think about the phrase, the more it makes sense, right?

Once a person gets out of the mindset of believing they know it all, they will move in the right direction.

Knowing that there's more information to learn puts your mental on a different level than others.

To detach from this toxic behavior, start with learning everything you need to know about the door you're trying to open. Without knowledge of such, there's no use. Success isn't relying on luck. It's knowing you're prepared and able to execute when the time is right.

Of course, when you take the time to learn and allow viable information to sink in, the next step is just as important.

Implementing what you know. This step can be difficult for a lot of reasons. Especially in the beginning, most will try it once, fail, and turn back. Great things take time and patience. Allow yourself to thrive on repetition, try things over and over and over and over again. This helps you figure kinks out, and allows you to discover different ways to approach the situation. Once you accomplish this, there's nothing you can't implement.

Let's say you become a pro at kicking doors down, what now? Unfortunately, that's nowhere near all you have to do to be successful because where there's a wooden door, there is a steel door right behind it. This will be where consistency comes into play. Life is a constant test, so gain tolerance for being tested. Make it a routine of knocking down those difficult doors standing in your way.

Educate Yourself

The most important thing in the twenty-first century is to educate yourself. This is critical because no one teaches the most important knowledge. For example, financial literacy isn't a requirement in most high schools in Memphis, Tennessee. To be honest, this hinders what children could know about money management. Children coming up should have the privilege to access this information.

Even without the school system, there's an opportunity to gain knowledge on any topic. One benefit that comes from educating yourself is that you're able to learn anything you need to know.

Educating yourself gives you a different attitude toward gaining new information. If you're attempting to gain control of your life, it's a must that you crash your basic routine. Seek to learn new knowledge daily. If it's hard for you to break from receiving the same dull information, then you're not willing to grow.

Below are a few tips that will help you feel more comfortable adjusting to new information.

It's Beneficial. New information is vital and beneficial to progress. If you're not progressing, you're regressing. Old information makes you complacent and stagnate. Start a new journey and learn something new every day. Pick up a book you have no clue about, and it will spark new ideas. New information also gifts you with a new perspective you can use to battle your indecisions. The more knowledge you have the better you'll be able to move through life.

Improve Communication. Educating yourself and reading allows an incline in communication. When you read, you're filled with knowledge you never had access to before.

Let Go of the Hood Mindset. The hood mindset, which is a toxic mindset that I wish I could cure myself. I know friends and family who think this mindset will benefit them in the long run. A hood mindset is a thought process that one can seldom alter and is a mind stuck in its way. We all know someone who has a hood mindset, and you know first-hand that it's tough to suggest anything new to them.

Being brought up in a hood environment can have a hold on a person. Mentally it's very painful because the influence is stronger than health. People will choose drugs over health, risk over health, and even sensation over health. This mind block is very heavy. It's the environment that has handcuffs on people. Have you ever heard the phrase, "What you see is what you get?" This statement is one hundred percent correct. If a person knows nothing else, it's hard to change. And, of course, it means what you see is what you get.

You don't have to be from the hood to have a hood mindset. It's more of a relatable phrase that indicates being trapped. When your mind is trapped, you're less likely to grow. Having a hood mindset is like a plant without sunlight. In this case, you need knowledge to sprout. Be open to new information and understand that you don't know everything. Life is an ongoing lesson, when you don't understand that you will suffer the same downfalls. It's not until you open your mind and receive new opportunities.

Stop Complaining

Listen up. If you're the type of person who complains about every single thing, I politely ask you to stop. You won't meet success behaving this way, you will encounter defeat. Of course, there's an easy fix to complaining. Like my favorite basketball player, Michael Jordan, once said, "Turn every situation into a positive situation." This takes some getting used to, it's a lifestyle change.

Your reality comes from the way you perceive things. If you're always downplaying, doubting, and assuming bad will happen then it will. There's a quote I hear often that goes, "Whether you think you can, or you think you can't… you're right." You are your mind. Mental health is as important as physical health. We all should deal with mental health accordingly. Spend more time with your mental health, and there will be sharper and more conscious decisions made in your life.

Remember there's always a solution, even when it seems like it's not. Complaining daily only sets you up for failure. When you're so used to complaining, it becomes routine. Instead of figuring out a solution, we hope complaining about it will work its magic.

Think of it like this. When we complain, it's typically about something we don't want. You focus your energy solely on your dissatisfaction with an event or situation that happened. Also, complaining is super contagious, you can easily get a crowd of people to nag. The energy you put out, you'll get right back, so focus on more positive thoughts.

Complaining won't help, it only brings you down. Below are tips to help seize complaining:

> ***Set a goal.*** Setting a goal will allow you to focus on accomplishing, not hoping. Hold yourself accountable and give yourself a task to complete. Action speaks louder than words, and there's no difference in this situation. Stop your complaining and do something about it.

#DontComplainChallenge. I created this challenge for myself because I felt as if I was doing a bunch of complaining and not enough action. This self-challenge has corrected my thought process and made me react more positively. Before a complaint rolls off your tongue, catch yourself and speak something positive instead of the negativity.

Get out of the sunken place. You're in a sunken place when you're not behaving like yourself. You feel as if you're lost, and that's when you temporarily lose your happiness. There's no light, your frustration is constantly poking you, and you don't know which way to go. These are signs of the sunken place. There's no gain for you in pleasing people because you will never be truly happy. People aren't truly happy, so do not lose yourself in making someone happy. When you have true happiness, it will show and you will benefit more. Get out of the sunken place.

The Person in the Mirror

I wrote this book to help y'all get off of y'all's asses. Stop wasting your time searching for answers when you already have them inside you. The person in the mirror is the most undefeated person you know. That person tells you exactly what you should hear. Whether it's the outrageous truth or a change you need to make. The question is, "Do you listen?"

To understand the person in the mirror, you must alter your mindset to take criticism well. The best criticism comes from one's self. I once told my wife, "If you think I'm tough on you, how hard do you think I go on myself? I'm my toughest critic because I've learned that if I tell myself before someone else does, they didn't tell me anything that I wasn't already aware of and I'm already ahead of the game to improve. I love improving.

Staring into the mirror is to take a ride within your soul. Get lost in yourself, because you must know yourself on this journey you're embarking on. There will be obstacles that will constantly test you, so you must know your flaws, your weaknesses, your strengths, what you're afraid of, and everything that makes you who you are. Doing this will instantly give you an advantage. Many people fear the need to know their weaknesses and their flaws, but wouldn't it be smart to know them so you can evolve yourself?

Once you know yourself inside out, confidence won't be a question. You gain the confidence trait when you're in tune with yourself. Here are a few ways to become in tune with yourself.

#1 Look at yourself objectively

#1 Be open to see other perspectives

#1 Follow your gut

#1 Be optimistic

#1 Meditate

I listed all the tips as number 1, to show that neither one of them are more important than the other.

#1 Look at yourself objectively. To learn how to view yourself objectively, you must let go of what you think you know. Viewing yourself objectively gives you a deeper and truer look into who you exactly are. Looking at yourself objectively differs greatly from being open to seeing other perspectives. By thinking objectively, you're intentionally placing yourself outside of your body to view yourself in a different aspect. As you probably know, you're biased to the way you are. Taking a step away can open your eyes to who you actually are. This allows you to make changes and evolve in areas that are needed.

#1 Be open to see other perspectives. Being open to the perspective of others is challenging for most people because we as people are super stubborn. When, in all actuality, listening is the greatest thing a person can do. Well, of course, if they want to advance in life. Listen and pay attention. That's the secret to receiving the information you never knew you needed. Learn to decipher between the words and listen for an opening that will enhance your circumstances.

#1 Follow your gut. Always follow your gut. This is a sign that you trust yourself. When you make decisions within your life, know that you're worthy. Never be afraid to decide, only prepare to deal with the results.

#1 Be optimistic. Being optimistic helps a person remain calm during a storm. A different storm presents itself every other day. Knowing it will get better will allow you to make it through.

#1 Meditate. I speak on this form of becoming in tune with yourself as an experience I've learned to love. Before I got into meditation, I procrastinated and didn't believe the benefits of it. I was wrong and you are, too. Meditating does great wonders for your body, but mainly your mind. It creates such a great vibe when it's done correctly. Your greatest ideas will come to mind, different opportunities will show, you will attract positivity, and you will feel motivated to push toward your goals.

Looking into the mirror is a brave thing to do, and not everyone has the guts to look themselves in the face and be honest. There's a point in life when you realize nothing is going to change unless it starts with you. People are so caught up in changing the people around them, they're wasting their precious time. Work on you and they will follow. After you've stared yourself up and down in the mirror, day after day, you will feel the benefits. The things that usually distract you won't even maintain your attention. Bad habits will be broken.

Accountability

To grow past your current level, you must learn to take on accountability. Yes, accountability can be humbling, embarrassing, and hurtful, but it's needed for progress. Accountability gives you understanding and control. Why did this happen? You made a decision and now it's time for you to own up to it! Sometimes, we lack fearlessness. We don't like to deal with the outcome. We gather these assumptions for how people may react or judge us. We fear perception instead of deliverance. We don't want to step on any toes or hurt the people close to us. But why should that be excepted when the truth heals? Why do we constantly filter ourselves? You're willing to hurt yourself instead of deciding to be real with one another.

Well, that stops here. Having accountability in your life shapes and molds your journey. When you find yourself in a rocky situation, what do you do most often? Search for an excuse? Find someone to blame it on? Belittle the power to control your own life? Or do you drown yourself in self-doubt and self-pity? If one of these is you, it's cool…you can overcome.

First, it starts with understanding what accountability actually means for your life. It's very simple. It means you're willing to accept responsibility. You're in charge of something as precious as your life and you never thought to be responsible? Your attitude will reform, and you will make different decisions for a more lasting journey.

Use these steps to sharpen your skills on accountability.

#1 Stop being toxic

#1 Pound excuses

#1 Stop hiding from the truth

#1 Search for ways to improve

Most of everything we have discussed so far is better said than done. Without hard work, effort, and accountability, none of these steps will work. Nothing comes to those who sit on their asses.

Stop being toxic. If this step is going to be a challenge for you, then you've come to the right place. Being toxic means you're infectious and harmful. If you're always thinking negative, reacting negative, and speaking negativity, then you're toxic. With this mentality, it will be impossible for you to take accountability for life because there's a thick barrier blocking you from greatness. A toxic individual will never notice their wrongdoings, which will lead them to never noticing the degrading effect their attitude is causing.

To escape the toxic mentality, I will suggest a cleanse. Change your morning routine, add exercising, meditation, things that will clear your mind, and give you a positive reaction. Stay away from social media first thing in the morning. There is nothing but opinions, toxic behaviors, negativity, and what's hot today.

Don't allow the vast majority to control your freshly woke brain. Altering your morning routine makes a lot of difference in how you will perceive your day. When you wake up, stay off that shit!

Pound excuses. Excuses are tools of the incompetent; they're used to build monuments of nothing and bridges to nowhere. Anything that stops you from completing your goal and you use it for the reason for not following through, is an excuse. It's easy to make up. It's simple to just throw an excuse in the air to keep yourself from accomplishing a goal.

"Uh, my legs are sore. So, I'll come back tomorrow to work out."

"I got off late, I'm tired, I can't work out."

"Man, I really got a lot of other stuff on my mind, I'll write tomorrow."

"I was busy."

Everything is an excuse! You're more than willing to achieve these things regardless of the circumstance. That's if you really want it bad enough. It's easy to become distracted. Don't use excuses to cover your sense of not having accountability.

You must pound excuses. For you to make it capable to pound excuses, you have to have constant battles with yourself and win. In the beginning, excuses are rarely an issue. It comes later when you need consistency to carry forward. When you're tired, not seeing any progress, and on the edge of giving up, you are tested the hardest. Be one step ahead mentally. Have accountability for your life.

You want to envision your dreams coming to a reality. Excuses won't get you that, having responsibility will. Goal chasing when tired, dealing with kids when tired, or performing a job task when you want to be at home in front of the television will get you those great results in the end. Positive results don't come from excuses. Excuses only get you stuck in one spot like a statue. Pound excuses!

Stop hiding from the truth. Accountability comes from knowing the truth. When hiding from the truth, it's easy to miss important details that will help you. Truth is reality. Why avoid reality? Be honest with yourself. Keep your eyes open, so you can see your opportunities. When we hide, we're on defense. We must be in alert mode.

It's a very simple step to overcome. Thrive on knowing the truth. If you hide often, be more aggressive in situations. Ask more questions to receive indications of what to do next, use trial and error to test things out, and take the truth head-on. It's only the truth!

Search for ways to improve. Searching to improve is a great sign you're on the correct path. It shows that you're humble and willing to learn. We don't know everything. Reading cut keys to any door. Reading broadens your horizon, as you receive different perspectives. If you search, you will find it.

Research! Any question you have has an answer. Search the web, read books, ask people in that particular field. Search endlessly. Tomorrow, when you find the answer, keep searching for more.

Read Between the Lines

Reading between the lines is a skill you must master. To read between the lines, you must be knowledgeable on the particular topic. This comes with everyday learning. Seeking knowledge on subjects you wouldn't normally have an interest in will immediately broaden your mindset. Most importantly, it makes you versatile.

Unsurprisingly, 2020 exposed plenty of one-track-minded people. It's time to read between the lines and develop a smarter approach to conversation. In conversation, people listen to respond. Let's do the opposite and listen to dissect. When you dissect a conversation properly, you find clues that are essential to you. Have you noticed that every time someone is speaking, the opposite person almost always replies selfishly? They'll reply with something like, "I remember the same thing happen to me when…" Instead, reply with questions that will increase your knowledge.

Not only…but also, I read between the lines through body language, emphasis, and eye contact. This is regarding face-to-face interaction. With text messaging, which is a more complex way, I find a trend with the words. I also use my imagination plus the knowledge I already have on the topic to extend my curiosity. This leads to more research, which leads to additional answers and questions. The day you stop learning is the day you die mentally.

Reading between the lines, you must be very attentive. Pay close attention; don't let irrelevant information distract you. Your level of focus should be at an all-time high. Of course, to program your mind to think this way takes repetition. Your mind should always be open to learn and seek new information. This is a skill you must use daily to master.

Context clues are almost identical to reading between the lines. Only being that it's for one particular word. When someone is speaking, it's almost necessary that you dissect their lingo and use context clues to figure out what they're actually trying to say. People have different meanings for certain words and topics, which is another reason it's vital to ask questions and listen.

Finally, reading between the lines can be an arduous task. Try not to assume anything. It's always great to ask questions to get down to the root of the answer. Let's say you assume one thing and you're wrong. Now you have false knowledge that will mislead you, and if you don't catch the flaw in time, it will lead to further misinformation. Becoming a master at reading between the lines takes practice, focus, and dedication. This skill is only useful if you seek knowledge daily and have prior knowledge of the subject you're attempting to dissect. Continue to learn and your life will forever grow.

Keep Up

Since you aren't competing with anyone, you have to keep up with yourself. This is a great way to remain humble, and if you're not humble, it is a trait I advise you to pick up. Check yourself before someone or something do it for you.

Your brain constantly sends ideas and signals your way causing you to react. To organize these thoughts, you must write your goals down to accomplish them. Keep up with your expectations. By doing this, you will save yourself the heartache of disappointment. Strategize your life and treat it like a business to keep up.

Be Realistic

To progress in life, you must keep it one hundred with yourself. Yes, I know you would like to become an overnight sensation or instantly become rich. It rarely works that way. It may seem like someone else's success happened overnight, but it didn't. That person was realistic and took initiative to work toward a goal.

Being realistic with yourself prepares you for potential criticism. No one will be able to rub you the wrong way because you've already been realistic with yourself. Now, instead of being behind the circumstance, you're in front of it and able to control it, which leads to better focus. Everything you do in life coincides.

Self-Discipline

Self-discipline leads to accomplishment. Being able to hold yourself accountable is one of the most important things on your journey. If you're not disciplined on your journey, you will never reach your full potential. Having structure leads to success. When you establish structure in your life, you're gaining control. Success isn't something that happens overnight or even out of nowhere. Do success on purpose and with self-discipline.

With self-discipline, there are a few important factors that play a huge role in reaching your destiny. Routine is one, the ability to say no is the second, and your motivation is the third. These factors are the reasons people rarely reach their goals or even reach them at all.

As easy as it's put, a person does need the will to fulfill their desires.

> ***#1 Routine.*** Creating a schedule structured toward your goal is as important as the goal itself. You must set your life up to receive what you want. Look at it as a strategy against the unpredictable outcomes of life. Many people attempt to wing their days and hope things drop out of the sky and reward them. Let's leave them alone and let them wait on their delusions, but if you're smart, you will at least control what you can and not wait on wonders.
>
> Repetition creates a habit. We want to get in the habit of living the life we want to create. If your ambitions are to become healthy and stronger, gear your routine toward eating correctly and attending the gym five days a week. Maybe you would like to become a rapper. You should focus on going to the studio to work on your craft to become a better lyricist. When you create a routine, you should focus on becoming the best. When

that's the mindset, you will plan accordingly and when executed you will receive the results.

#1 Learn how to say "No." At this point in our lives, our goals are very much important to us. We're not getting any younger, so we mustn't waste our time on foolishness. Most times, the best answer is no. People won't understand the seriousness of your goals unless you give that vibe that you're sternly invested. Honestly, a few people won't even respect what you're trying to accomplish. That's okay; it's not meant for them to understand. It's only for you, and in situations where you have to decide between your goal and "fun," that's your test.

Life has a humorous way of showing you what's more important to you. There's a line that everyone has used at least once in their life, "I'll do it tomorrow," or even saying, "One more time wouldn't hurt." That's the first sign that your goals aren't as important to you as you think they are. The day you push your goals to the side is the day you're disrespecting yourself.

Do you keep your word? When you tell someone you're going to do something for them, do you come through? Whether your answer is yes or no, the question is: Do you treat yourself the same way? Do you lie to yourself? I'm sure you have done it or might have heard someone else say, "This is my last blunt," but tomorrow they're back rolling up. They don't have any self-discipline. If you cannot stop lying to yourself, then you're not ready to accomplish your goals.

Tell your mind no. Your mind is extremely powerful, but it's only as strong as you allow it to be. You have to tell yourself no because something as small as stopping a bad habit can be in the way of your ambitions. When your best friends ask you to go out and you know your plans were to finish writing your book, say no. They will understand later when you have a best seller.

#1 Motivation. The person, people, things, or places driving you to accomplish your goals should be strong. When times get tough, you will need them. If your motivation isn't strong during times of doubt, you will crumble. Make sure the motivation that drives you will be worth it and makes you go harder when you feel like quitting. What drives you does have a lot to do with how far you will go. When I think of motivation, I think of my wife and child. For them, I will go beyond measures, and I will do anything it takes. I love when they're happy, so when I'm trying to accomplish my goals, I go harder so I can see the happiness on their faces when I reach my potential.

Find anything that motivates you to keep going. Make sure it's genuine and it can't be forgotten. Motivation comes from all aspects of life, so find anything that has a positive push on your life.

Apply self-discipline into your everyday life and watch how fruitful your world becomes. Use routine to structure your life, create a seriousness for your goals by saying no to things that don't benefit your ambitions. Last but not least, allow your motivation to carry you across the finish line of goal completion.

Allow Yourself to Have An Open Mind

Being open-minded comes from control. Some people are born with the gift and others must continue to practice mind control daily. It doesn't matter which way you look at it, practice makes perfect. Not only will practice strengthen your mind, but your thoughts will also be yours. The mind is the most important thing in the universe. Let's figuratively say you lose your mind tomorrow, what else are you useful for? The mind is a terrible thing to waste!

Another question would be, "How easily can you alter your mind?" I've always had my own strategic mindset. A person's opinion never changed the way I perceived anything. I always stuck to what I knew, unless it was straight out facts. But I will be truthfully honest… I had to stop myself from thinking that way. There was one thing I never listened to until recently. "Educate yourself." I wouldn't say I didn't take the statement seriously, I didn't know what educating yourself actually meant. It was only until I realized what I needed to know wasn't taught to me in school. I was furious; I didn't understand why the public school system so carelessly forgot to give us real education.

Once I finally came to my senses, I decided I had to educate myself. There are answers to the things you question. It's only a matter of knowing what to search for and how to manifest it in your direction. Just like you're reading this book, you should read many others. Learning never should stop, You shouldn't get complacent with your current position. You won't develop an open mind if you don't thoroughly educate yourself. Being educated is a complement to your natural knowledge. They work together to produce the answers that fit you.

Ask yourself, "Do I listen?" Regardless of your answer, the truth will set you free. Most of us aren't great listeners. We might be good listeners, but not great ones. If you want to become in control of your mind, you must be able to dissect. Here's how to analyze words that benefit you. Some might say this is a form of selective listening, but it's much deeper. Selective listening is only catching what matters to you and disregarding everything that doesn't. Now, being able to analyze words comes with practice. Most times, the answers you seek are those simple statements we overlook. Being able to dissect and listen to another person's words will allow you to ask the questions that will lead you closer to your answer.

The skill to dissect is very vital to your growth. Without it, it's difficult to understand your path. Dissecting different mindsets gives you an insight into other perspectives. Look at new perspectives as an investment in your life. In many ways, it benefits with the progress of your existence. You've been trapped long enough, exercise your brain more to become untrapped.

I use the term untrapped as a metaphor for being trapped. When you're brought up in a strong cultural city, it's easy for a person to become trapped. The lingo, the city norms, the people, and the stigmas have an unconscious impact on the way you perceive many things. It's more dangerous when you have no clue about this unconscious setback. Now is the time to change your behavior to receive a different outcome. You must be strong to become untrapped. It's definitely possible. Focus on expanding the most important muscle you have, your brain.

One of the important benefits of having an open mind is the many opportunities you will recognize. Many of us are going through or have gone through the phase of feeling as if nothing will go right for us. No matter how hard we try, doors just won't open, but no need to worry anymore. Having an open mind is the cheat code for receiving opportunities.

Look at it like this, having a one-track mind gives you access to pretty much one thing: a limited number of possibilities and outcomes. The unlimited opportunities that could lead to bigger and better are near you, but your vision isn't open enough to visualize it. Gaining more vision comes from educating yourself and dissecting new perspectives. There's a strategy that works well for me. It gives me an open mind, and I would like to share it with you.

First, clear your mind. Release tension and allow your mind to be genuinely grateful. Second, perform breathing techniques that will help bring calmness and understanding. The energy that comes from this approach allows positivity to circulate. Finally, make yourself naturally aware of your environment. Nature has the answers, because of the evolution that it provides. Be aware of the small things. They tend to have a bigger meaning.

Having an open mind is an everyday practice, and the more you study yourself you will witness the control you have. Your path is yours, continue to travel with confidence. There's no growth in staying still, you must move forward, and keep going. Learn along the way, educate yourself in every aspect you need. It's an investment that will quickly pay you back. Just like staying physically in shape is important, it's just as significant to exercise and feed your inner self. Observe the freeness you will receive just by developing a free mind. Open yourself, stop taking your ability for granted.

The Norm Isn't Correct

Just because everyone else is doing something, doesn't make it correct. Those who believe the norm is always correct, have a tough time doing creative things on their own. Leaders rarely grow when they're willing to always follow the norm of everyone else. You must have a question in your brain that triggers when you're doing the norm. "Am I following the norm and limiting myself?" Don't misconstrue what I mean when I say the norm isn't correct. I'm speaking directly to the leaders, and leaders create, not follow.

When following the norm, it makes us limited to what we can accomplish. The norm sets a boundary around your creativeness. I want you to reach outside of your boundary and expand your vision. Most people have a normal eye of everyday life, no imagination, or a broad vision. As a leader, you need telescope vision. See beyond.

Your vision should be broader because you want to improve daily. Without improvement, you're stagnating, and without a vision, you don't have a road map to your success. Most times in your life, you must be obsessive with your goals. There shouldn't be a day that goes by without your performing at least one task that will get you closer.

The norm isn't law, so I'm not implying you go out and break the law. I suggest that you break the cycle of the normal world, so you can one day produce a more fruitful life for you and your family.

We live in a fast pace world. It's easy to get caught up in life's complacency. It's about gaining control of your own mind and life. Slow yourself down, ask yourself questions, be obsessive about your goals, and be different.

> ***Slow yourself down.*** When life is moving fast, it's difficult to have control of your life. You might work plenty of jobs, taking care of your children, attempting to protect your social life, and you might even worry about

debt and bills. Take yourself out of this cycle daily, you need peace. Take social media breaks to rest your mind from the immediate news and opinions you receive. When your children are asleep or away, take advantage, and perform self-care routines. The most important thing is to gather your thoughts, slow your life down, and relax.

Ask questions. Ask yourself questions. When vibes aren't sitting well with your conscience, question the issue. Most times your conscience is communicating with you, just listen. Are you using your full potential in this situation, or are you sticking to the norm and limiting your chances? When you ask yourself questions, you are demanding a response. Be true to yourself, allow your mind to act with your own genuine response. No one else's opinion should be a factor. This way, you will receive a healthier outcome, because it's solely coming from you.

Be obsessive about your goals. I think about my goals all day. I think of ways I can accomplish them. I create systems on how I can gradually achieve them, and I analyze my effort. I'm obsessed with completing my goals. I'm obsessed with the steps that lead up to completing my goals. I'm just very passionate about my life and what I will make of it. I know I control my destiny, so I will do what it takes. Even with small goals, I put in the same effort. Be infatuated with your goals, high attention is needed.

Be different. We are who we are, we are individuals. There isn't a person in the universe who is the same as you. Even twins are different. I can't stress enough the importance of being yourself, because when you're being who you truly are you will always be different.

Being different sets you apart from anyone else. Even when people try to copy your style, there's nothing a person can do. Your style is yours, and no one can match or duplicate it.

Be Humble, Stay Humble

Be humble, stay humble means what it says. Let's be honest, we have our seasons when we're humble, and when we decide to get out of character. You start believing you're bigger than what you are, which is not a bad thing, I might add, but it's misleading because it blurs reality. Basically, we're undisciplined and any person who knows that can be dangerous.

It's easy to be humble when you feel as if you don't deserve it. It takes a turn when everything goes right. It's as if we get in a trance, we attempt to control it, but it gets out of hand. I asked myself, "How can I remain humble?" This is one of my toughest battles. I never get out of character to impress people, it's much more mental. I get comfortable, I get high off life, and I assume nothing can go wrong because I'm a genuine guy and I feel blessed. However, that has zilch to do with anything.

When we don't have it, we feel more obligated to get it. We're focused and we are attentive to details. We're humble and we listen. Looking pass the details is automatically negative in the operation. When we lose our humility, our character becomes childish. It's better to humble yourself before life does.

Finally, Let's get ahead of the curve. One thing that helps me stay humble is focusing on being aware. Actually, my most difficult goal is being mentally present. Especially when I'm always thinking about improving myself. I'm almost always searching for opportunities to progress. So, when I rest my mind and focus on the present situation, I'm greatly aware and humble.

Be Grateful (For the Now)

When I'm truly grateful, I receive more to be grateful for. When I say, "For the now," the meaning is supposed to set on you. Yes, you can be grateful for things that hasve happened to you before, but that's not as effective as being grateful present day. When I'm grateful for the present day, I feel at ease. That makes everything around me much better. When I say, "I'm grateful for my wife, my son, my mama, my sister, my brother, my family, and my friends," I get to appreciating everything. I become grateful for the car I can drive, the job I can go to, my furniture in my house, my house, and much more.

It's sort of like taking a few steps back and analyzing where you are in life. What have you created? Who's still around? Do you see any progress? Is this what you wanted? You unmistakably realize what you have. Being genuinely grateful says much about a person's awareness of their life.

Don't be afraid to let people know that you're grateful for them. People need to hear things like this, it makes the world a better place. Be grateful for who you know and what you have learned to get to the position you're in. Be grateful now and you will receive much more to be grateful for.

I'm Thankful

Now that we've come to the end of G.O.Y.A., I hope you are motivated to get off of your ass. I wrote this book to give inspiration, motivation, and a different perspective of hustling for what you want. This is mental hustling, how to think strategically and smart. Although I didn't write everything I know, I wrote everything that can get a person off their ass and see positive results.

The goal is to improve every day and be better than your yesterday self. You're not in competition with no one but yourself, and when you realize this, you will grow. Comparing your life to someone else's is detrimental to your destiny. Keep up with yourself and exert that focus on yourself.

Surround yourself with people who want to see you doing well. Gather around people who are better than you. A winner will use this opportunity to improve, not hate or envy. You are who you hang around. If you hang around ten broke people, then you're bound to be the eleventh. Vice versa, if you hang around ten rich people then, BAM! You're one of them.

Thank you for taking the time to improve yourself through perspective, experience, and tips I have provided for you. The information that I give in this book will only be words unless you apply them to your everyday life. I notice that people need guidance because there are tons of misleading information in the world. This book should prepare you to dissect good or bad information. Take what you've learned from this book and add it to other perspectives that arise throughout your journey. Thank you, once again, and I appreciate you for getting off of your ass.

Done.

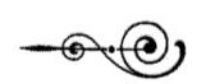

www.ingramcontent.com/pod-product-compliance
Ingram Content Group UK Ltd.
Pitfield, Milton Keynes, MK11 3LW, UK
UKHW040913300726
14061UKWH00007B/4

9 780578 841403